Committee for Development Policy

Policy Note

Achieving sustainable development in an age of climate change

United Nations
January 2009

DESA

The Department of Economic and Social Affairs of the United Nations Secretariat is a vital interface between global policies in the economic, social and environmental spheres and national action. The Department works in three main interlinked areas: (i) it compiles, generates and analyses a wide range of economic, social and environmental data and information on which States Members of the United Nations draw to review common problems and to take stock of policy options; (ii) it facilitates the negotiations of Member States in many intergovernmental bodies on joint courses of action to address ongoing or emerging global challenges; and (iii) it advises interested Governments on the ways and means of translating policy frameworks developed in United Nations conferences and summits into programmes at the country level and, through technical assistance, helps build national capacities.

Note

The designations employed and the presentation of the material in this publication do not imply the expression of any opinion whatsoever on the part of the Secretariat of the United Nations concerning the legal status of any country, territory, city or area or of its authorities, or concerning the delimitation of its frontiers or boundaries.

The term "country" as used in the text also refers, as appropriate, to territories or areas.

The designations of country groups are intended solely for statistical or analytical convenience and do not necessarily express a judgment about the stage of development reached by a particular country or area in the development process.

The views expressed in this publication are those of the Committee for Development Policy and do not necessarily reflect the opinions and policies of the United Nations.

United Nations publication
Sales No. E.08.II.A.16
ISBN 978-92-1-104592-5
Copyright © United Nations, 2009
All rights reserved
Printed by the United Nations
Publishing Section, New York

Foreword

At its tenth session, held in March 2008, the Committee for Development Policy continued to build on its previous work, addressing the issue of sustainable development by looking at the key channels through which climate change can undermine development and identifying potential strategies aimed at ameliorating any negative impact, with particular attention given to adaptation and mitigation policies, enhanced international cooperation (especially in finance and technology) and improved policy coherence.

The present Policy Note moves the discussion forward, examining in greater detail the various points made in the report on the Committee's tenth session (E/2008/33) and emphasizing the need for greater coherence in the different policies being pursued and, more broadly, for an integrated approach to sustainable development. The Policy Note is intended to contribute to the international discourse in 2009 and to help guide the building of a global consensus on the way forward.

Sha Zukang
Under-Secretary-General for Economic and Social Affairs
United Nations
January 2009

Acknowledgments

The present report reflects the collective views of the members of the Committee for Development Policy. The insights and ideas they contributed during its preparation are very much appreciated. Special gratitude must be extended to Hans Opschoor, Albert Binger and Tariq Banuri, who prepared background notes and other materials that served as important inputs for both Committee deliberations and this Policy Note.

Executive summary

Achieving the aims reflected in the international sustainable development agenda will require a drastic reduction in emissions in both developed and developing countries, in accordance with the principle of common but differentiated responsibilities and respective capabilities.

The cap-and-trade system, which provides for the buying and selling of carbon emission permits, remains the dominant approach to carbon mitigation. However, developing countries may derive greater benefit from an investment-based mitigation strategy that encourages the development and utilization of renewable energy alternatives and includes provisions for technology support, a regulatory framework, and research and education.

Capacity-building for the implementation of climate change adaptation measures is also essential, particularly in the most vulnerable developing countries, and will require action in the areas of poverty reduction, policy integration, and local engagement.

The operationalization of effective adaptation and mitigation strategies in developing countries requires substantial financial flows. Current allocations for activities aimed at addressing climate change are far below what are needed. The private sector will play the major role in financing the additional investment required, but support must also be provided by the public sector and through international cooperation.

Dealing with the challenges and opportunities emanating from the rapidly expanding carbon market requires technical and financial expertise and resources that may not be available in many developing countries. Those States lacking the necessary infrastructure and institutions will require assistance, especially if they wish to reduce their reliance on traditional fossil fuels and pursue clean energy options. The financial and technological aspects of sustainable development are intertwined, and barriers to access to the newest energy technologies should be removed.

Contents

Explanatory notes

The following abbreviations have been used in the present publication:

C	Celsius
CCS	carbon capture and sequestration
CER	certified emission reduction
CO_2	carbon dioxide
CO_2e	carbon dioxide equivalent
GHG	greenhouse gas
HIV/AIDS	human immunodeficiency virus/acquired immunodeficiency syndrome
ppm	parts per million
TRIPS	Agreement on Trade-Related Aspects of Intellectual Property Rights

Achieving sustainable development in an age of climate change

Introduction

The challenges of climate change for the implementation of the international development agenda were discussed by the Committee for Development Policy at its ninth session in March 2007; in its report, the Committee expressed concern over the lack of effective integration of climate-related issues into development action.[1] Since that time, the urgency of the issue has become greater and its relevance to development more manifest. The Committee has worked to identify specific elements that need to be addressed to meet sustainable development goals and to provide a concrete framework for operationalizing international cooperation within the parameters set by international agreements.[2]

At its tenth session, held after the adoption of the Bali Action Plan,[3] the Committee for Development Policy more closely examined the key channels through which climate change could undermine development and worked to identify potential strategies aimed at ameliorating any negative impact, with particular attention given to adaptation and mitigation policies, enhanced international cooperation (especially in finance and technology), and improved policy coherence.

---

1   United Nations, Committee for Development Policy, "Report on the ninth session (19-23 March 2007)", *Official Records of the Economic and Social Council, 2007, Supplement No. 33* (E/2007/33).

2   United Nations, agenda of the Expert Group Meeting on Strengthening International Cooperation for Development to Address the Climate Change Challenge, held in New York on 19 and 20 November 2007, available from http://www.un.org/esa/policy/devplan/egm_climatechange/climatechangeagenda.htm.

3   Secretariat of the United Nations Framework Convention on Climate Change, "Bali Action Plan" (advance unedited version), available from http://unfccc.int/files/meetings/cop_13/application/pdf/cp_bali_action.pdf.

Climate change: emerging challenges to sustainable development

Sustainable development is "a process of change in which the exploitation of resources, the direction of investments, the orientation of technological development, and institutional change"[4] are all compatible and enhance both current and future potential to meet human needs and aspirations. The notion of sustainability reflects concerns relating to the impact of development on the present generation, but it also requires ensuring that future communities have access to resources that will allow them to survive and prosper.

Prospects for sustainable development are undermined by a three-dimensional threat from climate change. The first dimension is climate change itself and its implications for human development, prosperity and health. The changing climate will have a direct impact on the progress made in achieving several key Millennium Development Goals, including Goal 7 (ensuring environmental sustainability), Goal 1 (eradicating extreme poverty and hunger), and Goal 6 (combating HIV/AIDS, malaria and other diseases).

Most seriously affected will be those countries that depend primarily on agriculture and have few opportunities for economic diversification and structural change. At the micro level, smallhold producers and others whose livelihoods depend on the exploitation of natural environmental resources are at greatest risk and are likely to experience a noticeable decline in their welfare.

It is anticipated that climate change will have a direct and significant adverse impact on economic growth in many arid and semi-arid countries in Africa. Most tropical and subtropical regions should expect lower crop yields; in some parts of Latin America, close to half of the agricultural land may be at risk of desertification and salinization.[5]

---

4 World Commission on Environment and Development, *Our Common Future* (New York: Oxford University Press, 1987), p. 9.

5 Secretariat of the United Nations Framework Convention on Climate Change, *Climate Change: Impacts, Vulnerabilities and Adaptation in Developing Countries* (Bonn: 2007), available from http://unfccc.int/files/ essential_background/ background_publications_htmlpdf/application/txt/pub_07_impacts.pdf.

The consequences of climate change may not be confined to individual countries. The world food supply is likely to decline if agricultural output losses suffered by countries adversely affected by climate change are not offset by increased production elsewhere.[6] Most studies indicate that if the global mean temperature rises by a few degrees or more, output growth will lag behind growth in global food demand, sending food prices upward.[7] Freshwater supplies are likely to diminish as a result of climate change, seriously undermining development and threatening basic human survival; mass migration from water-stressed areas is a very real possibility. Climate change can also have a negative impact on human health. Aside from contributing to the higher rates of malnutrition and related disorders that accompany reductions in the food supply, it can alter the distribution of some infectious disease vectors; in Africa, for example, changes in malaria incidence and prevalence patterns could aggravate the direct impact of climate change on economic growth.

The second dimension of the climate change threat is the spillover effects of climate-related policies implemented in the industrialized world. Developed countries play a dominant role in the world economy, and economic trends in these countries often have a global impact. The present credit crisis represents a case in point: preliminary estimates indicate that economic growth among developed countries declined from 3.8 per cent in 2007 to 1.8 per cent in 2008, and similar trends have been reported for developing countries and for the world as a whole (provisional figures indicate a decline from 7.3 to 5 per cent in the former and from 7.2 to 4.5 per cent in the latter).[8] Likewise, changes in climate or the adoption of

---

6   Although crop yield responses to climate change vary considerably, agricultural yields may increase in higher-latitude regions owing to temperature increases.

7   Intergovernmental Panel on Climate Change, "Summary for policymakers", in *Climate Change 2007: Impacts, Adaptation and Vulnerability—Contribution of Working Group II to the Fourth Assessment Report of the Intergovernmental Panel on Climate Change*, M.L. Parry and others, editors (Cambridge, United Kingdom: Cambridge University Press, 2007), p. 7, available from http://www.ipcc.ch/pdf/assessment-report/ar4/wg2/ar4-wg2-spm.pdf.

8   United Nations. "World economic situation and prospects 2008: update as of mid-2008" (advance unedited version) (updates *World Economic Situation and Prospects 2008*, United Nations publication, Sales No. 08.II.C.2), available from http://www.un.org/esa/policy/wess/wesp2008files/wesp08update.pdf.

policies to address climate change in developed countries can slow their rates of growth, with negative implications for international trade, financial flows, and commodity prices—and ultimately for growth in developing countries.

Slower economic growth is only one of the possible spillover effects of efforts to combat climate change among industrialized countries. Relevant sectoral policies can have serious consequences as well. For example, the shift to biofuel feedstock production stimulated by agricultural subsidies and other incentives is considered one of the factors contributing to the sharp increase in food prices in recent years, which has had a drastic impact on low-income net food importers, including many African countries. If biofuel sources constitute a substitute for, rather than a by-product of, normal agricultural production, the potential for food production could be permanently reduced at a time when demand is surging because of economic growth in consuming nations and supply is constrained by climate-related factors such as the recent drought in Australia and other climate-generated disruptions in major cereal-producing countries.

Another potential spillover effect would be the impact on trade of efforts by developed countries to ensure that production in other countries is not harmful to the environment. Many industrialized nations are transferring the production of metals and other goods with a high carbon footprint to developing countries and might undertake to ensure that production methods in the latter meet the highest international standards. Unless adequate arrangements are made for the financing and transfer of the clean technology needed to meet these standards, debilitating trade disputes could ensue.

The third dimension of the threat from climate change relates to the repercussions of the adaptation and mitigation activities undertaken by developing countries themselves. Development will be sustainable only if all countries in this group take action in both areas. However, positive results may only become apparent in the medium term; in the short term, there is a danger that the measures will be seen to have aggravated growth problems.

It is important for all stakeholders to recognize that addressing climate change can generate opportunities for economic growth and development. According to a recent report by the United Nations Environment

Programme, the clean energy market is growing rapidly, having attracted around US$ 148 billion in new funding globally in 2007. This represents a 60 per cent increase from the previous year, despite the deterioration in credit conditions in many parts of the world.[9]

The negative impact of climate change is already apparent at many levels. Mitigation efforts must be stepped up to further reduce emissions, and increased international cooperation is needed to facilitate the process of adaptation. Whatever the extent of the mitigative action taken in the wake of the Bali Action Plan, global warming will continue in the decades to come, as will the "fallout" from climate change (such as forced migration from drought-stricken areas). The need for adaptation, both to minimize the damage caused by climate change and to lower the cost of dealing with its consequences, will become more urgent. Much will depend on the magnitude of the impact and the rate at which the adverse effects of climate change materialize. It has become increasingly clear, however, that these have been underestimated and that much greater action will be needed in adaptation and mitigation than previously envisaged.

The key challenge is achieving policy coherence at both the national and international levels to ensure that any adverse effects from the three dimensions of the climate change threat do not interfere with the momentum of development, especially in developing countries.

The impact of climate change on vulnerable countries

In terms of development prospects, climate change may pose the greatest threat to the world's small island developing States and many of the least developed countries. As a group, these countries have contributed the least to overall greenhouse gas emissions but are the most vulnerable to, and have the least capacity to deal with, the impact of climate change. They

---

9   United Nations Environment Programme and New Energy Finance Ltd., *Global Trends in Sustainable Energy Investment 2008* (DTI/1066/PA), available from http://sefi.unep.org/fileadmin/media/sefi/docs/publications/Global_Trends_2008.pdf (accessed on 1 July 2008).

tend to be more susceptible than other countries to the adverse effects of atmospheric and oceanic warming, changes in precipitation, and extreme events; vulnerabilities within this context relate mainly to freshwater supplies, agriculture and food security, health, ecosystems, and coastal zones.

Over the long term, if warming trends contribute to a steady rise in sea level, some small island developing States may face complete collapse. According to the Intergovernmental Panel on Climate Change, "sea-level rise will exacerbate inundation, erosion and other coastal hazards, threaten vital infrastructure, settlements and facilities, and thus compromise the socio-economic well-being of island communities and States."[10] By the end of the twenty-first century, sea level is expected to rise by between 0.19 and 0.58 metres, though a number of climate models indicate that there will be geographic variations.

Climate change is dramatically affecting weather patterns in many areas. Evidence indicates that the number of Category 4 and 5 storms has increased globally since 1970. Countries that had previously been unaffected by cyclonic events, such as Grenada, have suffered catastrophic damage as the geographic range of hurricane activity has expanded. For the small island developing States as a group, there has been a noticeable increase in the number of reported natural disasters over the past several decades (see figure 1).

One issue requiring urgent attention in the small island developing States is the impact of global warming on existing freshwater sources. In many coral atoll countries, freshwater is available from groundwater lenses that are dependent on rainfall and are extremely fragile. More frequent or longer-lasting droughts can reduce the availability of water. Similarly, with stronger and more frequent storms occurring, the lenses can become contaminated with seawater, compromising water quality.

Africa is extremely vulnerable to the impact of climate change. Projected changes in precipitation will exacerbate an already stressed situation; extreme poverty and other major development challenges seriously limit the

---

10   N. Mimura and others, "Small islands", in *Climate Change 2007: Impacts, Adaptation and Vulnerability—Working Group II Contribution to the Fourth Assessment Report of the Intergovernmental Panel on Climate Change*, M.L. Parry and others, editors (Cambridge, United Kingdom: Cambridge University Press, 2007), p. 689.

continent's adaptive capacity. Global warming in this region will primarily affect water resources, agriculture and food security, natural resource management and biodiversity, and human health. Many parts of Africa are already experiencing a major deficit in food production, and if soil moisture declines, as predicted, the situation will worsen. Food-insecure countries are more likely to be adversely affected by climate change. By 2020, crop yields could decline by as much as 50 per cent in some countries.[11]

Figure 1
The incidence of natural disasters in small island developing States, 1970-2006

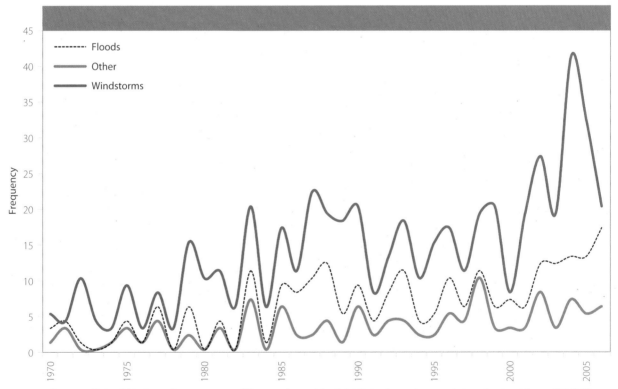

Source: United Nations, Department of Economic and Social Affairs, based on statistics obtained from *EM-DAT: Emergency Events Database*, available from http://www.emdat.be.

Note: "Other" denotes disasters resulting from tidal waves (including tsunamis), volcanic eruptions, mudslides, landslides, earthquakes and drought.

11   M. Boko and others, "Africa", in *Climate Change 2007: Impacts, Adaptation and Vulnerability—Working Group II Contribution to the Fourth Assessment Report of the Intergovernmental Panel on Climate Change*, M.L. Parry and others, editors (Cambridge, United Kingdom: Cambridge University Press, 2007), pp. 433-467.

Among the least developed countries in Asia, the impact of climate change will be manifested in an enhanced hydrological cycle and increased rainfall; models predict an annual mean increase in precipitation of about 3 per cent by 2020 and 7 per cent by 2050. For central Asia, an increase in winter precipitation and a decrease in summer precipitation are projected. As precipitation levels in this area are already low, some countries are likely to experience severe water stress and drought. Rice-growing areas might be affected, and the consequent declines in yield would have a significant impact on agricultural trade, economic growth, and the achievement of development goals in certain parts of Asia.

Some developed countries are already investing in adaptation; however, developing countries—in particular small island developing States and least developed countries—have limited technical and financial resource capacities and therefore face far greater challenges in implementing adaptation measures. Overcoming these challenges constitutes a critical priority, given the level of exposure and extreme vulnerability within the developing world to the potentially adverse effects of climate change. Developing countries urgently need to strengthen their capacities to assess their vulnerabilities and deal with climate change risks, and to develop adaptation strategies that are fully integrated into development planning at the national, regional and international levels.

Sustainable development and climate change: towards an integrated approach

The Parties to the United Nations Framework Convention on Climate Change pledged to work towards achieving the "stabilization of greenhouse gas concentrations in the atmosphere at a level that would prevent dangerous anthropogenic interference with the climate system … within a timeframe sufficient … to enable economic development to proceed in a sustainable manner".[12]

---

[12]   United Nations Framework Convention on Climate Change, article 2, available from http://unfccc.int/ resource/docs/convkp/conveng.pdf.

When climate change is acknowledged as a key issue within the wider sustainable development context, it becomes imperative that incentives be provided for sustained economic growth along pathways that not only enhance capabilities and options among people and societies but also facilitate a major, or even total, shift away from carbon fuel use as well as the strengthening of adaptive capacities in developing countries.

The challenges faced by developing countries in achieving sustainable development are considerable. Their overriding policy priority is economic growth, which entails expanding the reach of energy and infrastructure and making them available to a larger proportion of the population. At present there are wide disparities between developed and developing countries in terms of unmet energy needs. About 1.6 billion people, or 32 per cent of the population in developing countries, do not have access to electricity; among industrialized countries and economies in transition, the corresponding figure is 8 million, or 0.5 per cent of the population (see table). Economic growth and development are typically associated with increased demand for natural resources in general and for energy resources in particular. Reorienting this growth trajectory requires investment in building new infrastructure, new capacities, and new institutions.

In industrialized countries, the main policy approach to dealing with global climate change has been the cap-and-trade system, reinforced by national regulations, subsidies and incentives to promote non-polluting investment and activities and encourage research and development. While there are several important criticisms of the cap-and-trade method (the upshot being that emissions have continued to rise), it is possible that this approach will become more effective in developed countries once enforceable targets are adopted, as it is consistent with the monitoring and regulatory capacities of these countries. However, relying exclusively on this approach is not practical if development is to be achieved. Making the use of carbon sources more costly—whether through increased oil prices, the application of a carbon tax, or dealings within emissions markets—is regressive in nature and will ultimately halt development.

Table
Electricity access in 2005

Regions	Total population (in millions)	Population without electricity (in millions)	Electrification rate (percentage)
Africa	891	554	37.8
North Africa	153	7	95.5
Sub-Saharan Africa	738	547	25.9
Developing countries in Asia	3 418	930	72.8
China and East Asia	1 951	224	88.5
South Asia	1 467	706	51.8
Latin America	449	45	90.0
Middle East	186	41	78.1
Developing countries	4 943	1 569	68.3
Economies in transition and OECD countries	1 510	8	99.5
World	6 452	1 577	75.6

Source: International Energy Agency, *World Energy Outlook 2006* (Paris: 2006), p. 567.
Note: Totals may not add due to rounding.

Addressing climate change requires effective and sustained collaboration between industrialized and developing countries. Currently, about half of the world's carbon emissions come from industrialized countries, where 20 per cent of the global population is responsible for about 80 per cent of overall economic output. The remaining half comes from developing countries, which account for the vast majority (80 per cent) of the global population but generate only one fifth of gross world product. Emissions of CO_2 far exceed the earth's absorptive capacity, which is estimated at about 5 billion metric tons of carbon dioxide equivalent (CO_2e) per year.[13] Annual global fossil fuel emissions of CO_2 alone are now over

---

[13]   Nicholas Stern, *The Economics of Climate Change: The Stern Review* (Cambridge, United Kingdom: Cambridge University Press, 2007).

27 billion metric tons. Over the next century, the emissions of all countries have to be reduced by 80 to 95 per cent, depending on the group as well as the target selected, if global warming is to be contained at 2° C. Neither developed nor developing countries can resolve this crisis by themselves; the emissions of both groups must be radically curtailed.[14]

Given the requirements outlined above, the most constructive response would be to set up a global infrastructure investment programme that sent the appropriate market signals to the private sector and levelled the playing field for alternative energy technologies so that targets could be achieved and adaptation facilitated.

Mitigation costs are expected to total around 1-2 per cent of global economic output (estimated at US$ 48 trillion in 2006). As indicated in the box below, actual outlays will depend on a number of factors, including reduction targets and time frames. It should be emphasized that climate change will continue under most of the scenarios considered, though more slowly than would otherwise be the case; consequently, adaptation measures are also required.

Annex I Parties to the United Nations Framework Convention on Climate Change[15] will need to take the lead in developing mitigation options and be ready to provide the kind of financial and technological support that enables industrializing developing countries to participate in mitigation efforts (as envisaged in the Bali Action Plan) while also pursuing their development and energy-related goals. Several developing countries, including those that are economically most vulnerable, have prepared national adaptation plans of action. These plans need to be implemented after any necessary updating and refinement, with international support provided in the form of funding, technology transfer and capacity-building.

14   Tariq Banuri, "Twelve theses: sustainable development agenda for climate change", available from http://www.un.org/esa/policy/devplan/egm_climatechange/banuri.pdf.

15   Including industrialized countries that were OECD members in 1992 as well as countries with economies in transition (see http://unfccc.int/parties_and_observers/items/2704.php).

Confronting climate change:
How much does mitigation cost?

Estimating mitigation costs is a complex exercise, not least because there are so many uncertainties and unknowns. Carbon concentration levels and the rate at which they are to be stabilized constitute a point of reference, however.

The emission reduction scenarios referenced in the Bali Action Plan highlight different options and their implications. In a scenario in which CO_2e concentrations total 445-490 parts per million (ppm) in 2100, emissions would have to peak between 2000 and 2015 in order for the increase in global mean temperature over pre-industrial levels to remain within the range of 2.0° C to 2.4° C, and there would have to be a 50-85 per cent reduction in 2000 global emissions by 2050. In another scenario, where CO_2e concentrations measure 855-1130 ppm in 2100, emissions would peak during the period 2060-2090, and the global mean temperature would have risen by 4.9° C to 6.1° C. The latter scenario implies a 90-140 per cent increase in emissions.[a] Costs will depend not only on the nature and extent of the mitigation efforts, but also on when and where emissions are to be reduced and the degree of participation among other countries.

The figure below provides an idea of the projected costs of stabilizing CO_2e at different levels by 2100. Cost predictions vary considerably, even for stabilizing greenhouse gas (GHG) concentrations at the same level; stabilization at 450 ppm CO_2e, for example, could require outlays ranging from less than US$ 400 trillion to around US$ 1,800 trillion.[b] With higher stabilization targets, costs are likely to be substantially lower; as shown in the figure, projected costs for all scenarios in which CO_2e levels are stabilized at 750 ppm are well under US$ 200 trillion.

While acknowledging the difficulties in assessing the orders of magnitude involved, a recent United Nations Framework Convention on Climate Change report indicates that between US$ 200 billion and US$ 210 billion in additional investment will be required in 2030 to restore GHG emissions to current levels.[c] Roughly half of the mitigation efforts will need to be carried out in developing countries, whose gross domestic product collectively accounts for less than one fifth of the world total.

The Bali Action Plan states that a "long-term global goal for emission reductions" should be one of the agreed outcomes of the forthcoming negotiations; however, the range of mitigation scenarios referenced in the Plan is very broad. As shown above, one option requires immediate and urgent action by all countries to limit the

a Intergovernmental Panel on Climate Change, "Technical summary", in *Climate Change 2007: Impacts, Adaptation and Vulnerability—Contribution of Working Group II to the Fourth Assessment Report of the Intergovernmental Panel on Climate Change*, M.L. Parry and others, editors (Cambridge, United Kingdom: Cambridge University Press, 2007), p. 15.

b Projections are in trillions of 1990 United States dollars.

c Secretariat of the United Nations Framework Convention on Climate Change, "Report on the analysis of existing and potential investment and financial flows relevant to the development of an effective and appropriate international response to climate change", prepared for the Fourth Workshop of the Dialogue on Long-Term Cooperative Action to Address Climate Change by Enhancing Implementation of the Convention, held in Vienna from 27 to 31 August 2007 (Dialogue Working Paper 8, 8 August 2007).

rise in global mean temperature to about 2° C, while another does not seem to imply the need for drastic action but would result in what many experts consider an existential threat to the planet—an increase in global mean temperature of about 5° C.

Without a precise definition of the ultimate objective, it is difficult to determine how resources might best be divided between and directed towards mitigation and adaptation. If GHG output is allowed to increase steadily until about 2050, necessitating higher stabilization levels for CO_2e in the atmosphere, climate change will proceed, and its adverse consequences—including more frequent hurricanes and tornadoes, the diminution of water supplies, reduced agricultural yields, and increased flooding in the coastal regions—will become more serious. Addressing these problems will require more resources than would have been the case had greater effort been devoted to mitigation. Given all the variables and uncertainties involved, adaptation costs are even harder to project than mitigation costs.

The projected cost of stabilizing CO_2 emissions, 1990-2100

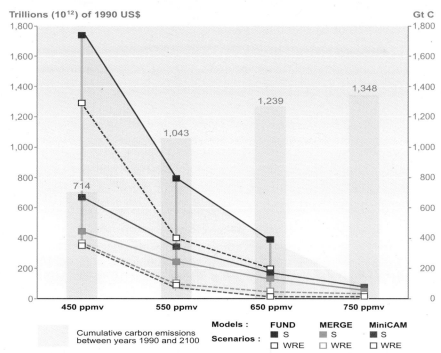

Source: Intergovernmental Panel on Climate Change, "Graphics, presentations and speeches", figure 7-3, in *Climate Change 2001: Synthesis Report*, available from http://www.ipcc.ch/graphics/graphics/2001syr/large/08.23.jpg (accessed on 21 January 2008).

The need for mitigation in achieving sustainable development

Achieving the aims reflected in the international sustainable development agenda, including the Millennium Development Goals, will be impossible unless carbon emissions are drastically reduced. Key factors to consider in a sustainable development approach to mitigation include equitable emission targets, energy transition, the impact of consumption patterns in other countries, forestry and land use, mitigation regimes, and investment approaches to mitigation.

Equitable targets

The concentration of greenhouse gases (GHGs) in the atmosphere is currently 379 parts per million (ppm) CO_2e, compared with 280 ppm before the Industrial Revolution.[16] Factored into CO_2e calculations are estimated levels of CO_2 and other GHGs, with the latter accounting for about 23 per cent of the climate change potential.

It is not enough to slow down or even halt the increase in emissions; GHG concentrations must be reduced to a fraction of what they are today in both developed and developing countries. This represents an unprecedented challenge—one that will require drastic changes in the way the world operates.

The Bali Action Plan recognizes "that deep cuts in global emissions will be required to achieve the ultimate objective" of the United Nations Framework Convention on Climate Change and emphasizes the urgency of the situation.[17] However, no specific targets or time frames for reducing emissions beyond 2012 have yet been established.

16   Intergovernmental Panel on *Climate Change, "Summary for policymakers", in Climate Change 2007: Impacts, Adaptation and Vulnerability—Contribution of Working Group II to the Fourth Assessment Report of the Intergovernmental Panel on Climate Change*, M.L. Parry and others, editors (Cambridge, United Kingdom: Cambridge University Press, 2007), p. 8, available from http://www.ipcc.ch/pdf/assessment-report/ar4/wg2/ar4-wg2-spm.pdf.

17   Secretariat of the United Nations Framework Convention on Climate Change, "Bali Action Plan" (advance unedited version), Decision -/CP.13, preamble paragraph 4, available from http://unfccc.int/files/meetings/cop_13/application/pdf/cp_bali_action.pdf.

Global emission reduction targets will need to be regionally differentiated. Existing proposals that, for example, call for a 50 per cent reduction in 1990 emissions by the year 2050 may require developed countries to shoulder 70 per cent of the burden, which implies total emission cuts of 30 per cent for developing countries. However, because the population in developing countries is expected to double during the period 1990-2050, such cuts would amount to per capita reductions in developing countries close to those suggested for developed countries.[18] Clearly, this does not reflect the principle of differentiated responsibilities. Larger reductions, which are necessary to ensure that emissions are stabilized at a level that will prevent the global temperature from rising by more than 2° C, would leave developing countries with very little room to manoeuvre in terms of increasing their consumption of energy from traditional sources (see figure 2). In any case, significant cuts in developing countries would pose a major challenge given the need to reconcile mitigation efforts with the necessary growth in energy consumption.

Energy transition

The energy sector is enormously important within the present context, as it is responsible for over three quarters of total GHG emissions but is also inextricably linked to economic activity and the fulfilment of human needs. Access to energy is distributed very unevenly both within and between countries. As mentioned previously, per capita energy consumption in developing countries averages less than a fifth of that in industrialized countries (see figure 3). A key element of the sustainable development agenda is the enhancement of energy availability in the longer run.

Per capita energy consumption in the developing world is expected to increase fourfold to sixfold over the next century. In its Reference Scenario, the International Energy Agency projects that the world's primary energy needs will rise by 55 per cent between 2005 and 2030, growing at an average rate of 1.8 per cent a year. It is predicted that around US$ 22

---

18   Paul Baer and others, *The Right to Development in a Climate Constrained World: The Greenhouse Development Rights Framework*, revised second edition (Berlin: Heinrich Boll Foundation, November 2008), available from www.ecoequity.org/docs/TheGDRsFramework.pdf.

trillion will have to be invested in the supply infrastructure to meet global energy demand by the end of this period. This can be compared with gross world product of about US$ 48 trillion in 2006 and official development assistance totalling US$ 104 billion in 2007. The Agency maintains that "mobilizing all this investment will be challenging".[19]

Figure 2
Per capita emissions from fossil fuel combustion, 2000-2050

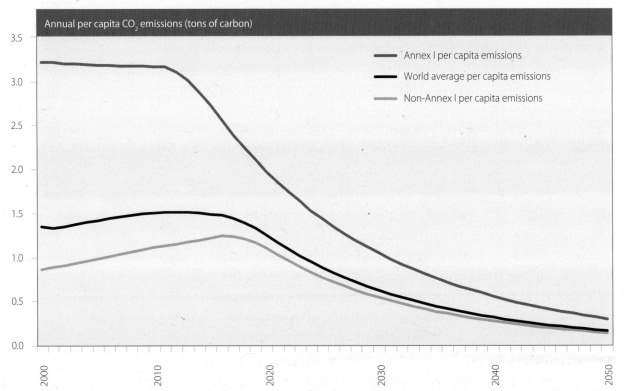

Annual per capita CO_2 emissions (tons of carbon)

— Annex I per capita emissions
— World average per capita emissions
— Non-Annex I per capita emissions

Source: Paul Baer and others, *The Right to Development in a Climate Constrained World: The Greenhouse Development Rights Framework*, revised second edition (Berlin: Heinrich Boll Foundation, November 2008), available from www.ecoequity.org/docs/TheGDRsFramework.pdf.

Note: Among industrialized countries and economies in transition (Annex I Parties to the United Nations Framework Convention on Climate Change), the figure for 2050 indicates a 90 per cent decline in 1990 emission levels.

19   International Energy Agency, *World Energy Outlook 2007: Executive Summary— China and India Insights* (Paris: IEA Publications, 2007), p. 4, available from http://www.iea.org/Textbase/npsum/WEO2007SUM.pdf.

Figure 3
Energy use per capita, 2005

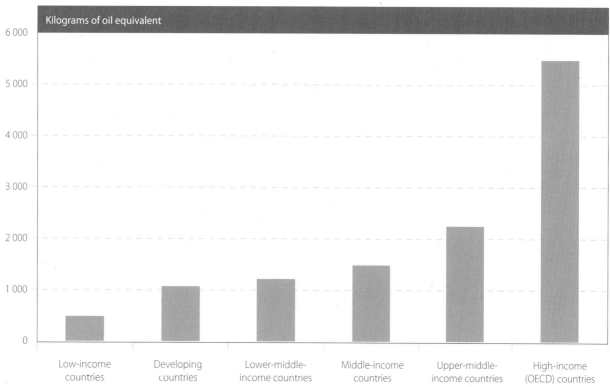

Kilograms of oil equivalent

Low-income countries | Developing countries | Lower-middle-income countries | Middle-income countries | Upper-middle-income countries | High-income (OECD) countries

Source: Based on figures obtained from the *World Development Indicators* online database (accessed on 28 August 2008).

There are significant differences between fossil sources of energy and renewable alternatives in terms of both cost and convenience. Shifting to cleaner alternatives without jeopardizing development or equity goals would be impossible for even the most dynamic economies without external financial support and technological assistance.

Switching to nuclear energy constitutes an example of the level and type of assistance required as well as the complexity of the issues at stake. Nuclear power plants can cost more than US$ 1 billion, and the long lead times, technology transfer and safety requirements (especially in earthquake zones), and limited availability of sufficient expertise to construct new plants on the scale needed would seem to call into question the viability of the nuclear option. While nuclear power is a known technology, the capital and running costs associated with other new and renewable sources of energy cannot be estimated with any degree of accuracy. A major challenge will be convincing the private sector in developing countries to invest in clean energy industries when dirtier alternative sources are readily available and probably cheaper.

The original United Nations Framework Convention on Climate Change, in paragraph 3 of article 4, establishes a guiding principle for determining financial assistance requirements, whereby developed countries are to "meet the agreed full incremental costs" of a range of measures undertaken by developing countries in complying with their obligations under article 12, paragraph 1, of the Convention. Again, the orders of magnitude are very large. For instance, it is estimated that the capital costs for a carbon capture and sequestration (CCS) plant would be US$ 1 billion higher than those for a conventional plant, and carbon capture would increase the operational cost of electricity generation in coal plants by 35-60 per cent.[20] Retrofitting existing plants to capture emissions would be more costly than applying CCS technology to new integrated gasification combined cycle technology plants.

Considerable thought will have to be given to the question of "incremental costs" if this is to be the principle governing financial transfers. Will the benchmark be the dirtiest fuels, such as coal, and the comparison made with solar, wind or nuclear energy? Will such assistance cover differences in the capital costs and/or the running costs of the plants? The latter are often higher for energy sources such as wind or solar power than for conventional sources, but they should decline over time with advances in technology and as the world acquires more experience in the use of the newer technologies.

Essentially, a reconceptualization of the international development and climate change agendas would be necessary for the design of a technological, financial, and institutional structure that would support and sustain the shift from fossil fuel dependence to a renewable energy trajectory.

20   United Nations Development Programme, *Human Development Report 2007/2008—Fighting Climate Change: Human Solidarity in a Divided World* (New York: Palgrave Macmillan, 2007), available from http://hdr.undp.org/en/media/HDR_20072008_EN_Complete.pdf.

Consumption and emission targets

In determining equitable reduction targets to achieve sustainable development, one important question relates to the attribution of liability for production-related environmental pressures (including climate change). Consumption follows production in its various stages, but production and consumption take place in different locations. Using a product life-cycle approach, the environmental repercussions of producing various goods (such as GHG emissions) will need to be incorporated in the calculations of environmental pressures related to the consumption of these goods. Such assessments will have a bearing on the calculation of equitable targets.

In a globalizing world with rapidly expanding trade flows, it is likely that the economic structure of countries will continue to change and evolve. Developed countries will become increasingly service-oriented, shifting away from high-emission industries such as iron, steel, aluminium, chemical, glass, and paper production. "Outsourcing" the production of fossil-fuel-intense, high-emission goods to developing countries has been occurring for some time. However, once developed countries enact provisions that require these industries to pay a price for their carbon emissions, disputes could arise between producers in developed countries and those in developing countries, with the former claiming that the latter have an unfair advantage in not having to pay for their emissions.

Forestry and land use

Land use and deforestation are responsible for roughly a quarter of global greenhouse gas emissions.[21] The inclusion of emissions resulting from land

---

21 Deforestation was responsible for about 17 per cent of GHG emissions in 2004. Data include CO_2 emissions from deforestation, from decay (decomposition) of above-ground biomass that remained after logging and deforestation, and from peat fires and the decay of drained peat soils. Agriculture generated another 13 per cent of emissions that year. The figure includes agricultural waste burning and savannah burning (non-CO_2 emissions). CO_2 emissions and/or removals from agricultural soils are not included here. See G.J. Heij and others, "Technical summary", in *Climate Change 2007: Mitigation—Contribution of Working Group III to the Fourth Assessment Report of the Intergovernmental Panel on Climate Change*, B. Metz and others, editors (Cambridge, United Kingdom: Cambridge University Press, 2007), available from http://www.ipcc.ch/pdf/assessment-report/ar4/wg3/ar4-wg3-ts.pdf.

use conversion makes for a very different ranking of countries according to their overall emissions. Land use conversion to allow the production of other crops or the introduction of larger-scale production systems (such as plantations) can result in increased employment and income. However, this often involves trade-offs in terms of the rights and socio-economic prospects of local communities that made their living from the previous land use patterns. One issue with particular relevance to sustainable development is the large-scale shift in land use towards the production of biomass for fuel generation, as evidence suggests that there may be significant trade-offs related to food security and food prices. Issues such as these highlight the importance of using an integrated approach to address challenges linked to climate change.

Mitigation regime: combining different options

The three main, though not mutually exclusive, policy approaches to dealing with mitigation in general and with environmental "bads" in particular include creating a quasi-market to define emission rights (such as the cap-and-trade system); applying taxes and incentives to internalize the external costs of emissions and the benefits of cleaner alternatives; and dealing directly with the causes of the "bads" through regulation. All of these options imply some level of public regulation. The first two rely on the self-correcting capacity of the market (following a redefinition of property rights or the cost conditions under which they operate), while the third involves more formal regulatory procedures as even corrected markets may not generate acceptable solutions (or do so within an acceptable time frame). A number of other options that may be more effective in the developing country context appear to have been disregarded in policy discussions. Foremost among these are research and development funding, the regulation of fuel portfolios as well as emission levels, economic incentives, technological support, and education. It is essential, given the urgency of the situation, that the complementarity of these alternatives be recognized and that a multiplicity of approaches be incorporated into mitigation regimes.

The investment approach to mitigation

Development paths differ in terms of their impact on the climate, just as diverse climate policies affect development trajectories in different ways. If sustainable development is to be achieved, countries will no longer have the option of following a traditional fossil-fuel-dependent development path. Effecting the energy transition described earlier requires an innovation- and investment-oriented approach to mitigation, complemented by institutional capacity-building; the successful model of institutional support for the green revolution in South Asia could guide efforts to enhance the mitigation capacity of developing countries in particular. There are strong win-win possibilities for both developed and developing countries in terms of increased energy efficiency; for the latter group, however, care must be taken to factor in the rapid growth in the energy sector as consumption requirements continue to rise.

The facts presented thus far suggest that the most critical element of the mitigation strategy for developing countries is the redirection of investment towards renewable energy alternatives. In spite of the complexities and uncertainties involved, this approach offers invaluable development-related opportunities. As developing countries undertake a broad range of development activities that contribute to greenhouse gas abatement, they are likely to gain technological know-how, market insights, and experience in the adoption of relevant policy instruments. Similarly, private investors, civil society actors, and local communities, compelled and/or supported by the pertinent policy measures, will acquire the knowledge and capacity to eventually undertake actions addressing climate change autonomously. The deployment of such options will lead to a reduction in unit costs, making it easier for countries at all levels of development to adopt them without negative implications for the sustainable development agenda. Experience in this area can also create market opportunities for developing countries. The development of adequate technology for producing ethanol from sugar cane in Brazil (together with the related production of ethanol-only and hybrid cars) is a case in point.

Adaptation and sustainable development

In many parts of the developing world, but particularly in the least developed countries, climate change has a negative impact on people's livelihoods, weakening their resource base and limiting their options and capabilities. It may also erode their capacity to adapt. Steps must be taken to increase resilience to climate change if development objectives are to be met. Successful adaptation will require action in the areas highlighted below.

Poverty and adaptation

Vulnerability to climate change is closely linked to poverty through the following: climate-related risks to securing and sustaining well-being; poverty-related constraints on adaptive capacity; and poverty-related determinants of exposure. These factors need to be addressed if poverty reduction and adaptation efforts are to reinforce one another. Successful adaptation requires a more equitable distribution of economic growth, access to resources, greater equity between genders and social groups, and increased participation in local decision-making (especially by the poor).

Local engagement and adaptive capacity

Awareness of local vulnerabilities to climate change is emerging, as are coping strategies. However, there is a need to engage with local residents and grass-roots groups to enhance awareness and identify the most effective strategies. Local adaptive capacities—influenced at the individual and community levels by resource availability and by access to social and economic networks, entitlements, institutional support, education and technology—are unevenly distributed within and between societies and need to be strengthened.

Policy integration and coherence at the national level

Because adaptation is seen primarily as an environmental issue, there is a tendency to compartmentalize climate change policies and place them under the direct purview of environmental or natural resource protection ministries. As a result, most Government officials in other ministries do not consider addressing climate change a development issue. This constitutes one of the main institutional barriers to mainstreaming adaptation in development policies. Adaptation must be integrated not only into development policy in general but also into policy areas such as poverty reduction, rural development, disaster risk management, water resources, health, and infrastructure investment. Similarly, sustainable development policies aimed at improved governance and natural resource management are vital to climate change adaptation.

International cooperation and policy coherence

The Bali Action Plan establishes a basic framework for international cooperation on climate policy in the context of sustainable development, linking mitigation actions in developing countries to financial, technological, and capacity-building support from industrialized countries; cooperation in expanding adaptation capacity in the most vulnerable countries; and the provision of incentives to link adaptation to sustainable development policies. Because climate change is a global phenomenon, international cooperation is the only means through which sustainable development can be achieved. Coalitions involving all stakeholders constitute the most effective way to ensure optimal emission reductions.

International cooperation in finance

The box presented earlier includes rough estimates of the financial resources needed for adaptation and mitigation in developing countries. Presently, about 82 per cent of the costs are being financed domestically among non-Annex I Parties, with Government participation averaging just over 12 per cent. The share of foreign direct investment in investment financing is 14 per cent on average, while official development assistance accounts for about 1 per cent.[22] The private sector is already playing a major role and is

---

22 In sub-Saharan Africa, Government participation in mitigation and adaptation activities averages 26 per cent, while foreign direct investment and official development assistance respectively account for 5 per cent and 2 per cent of the total.

expected to continue to supply most of the additional investment financing needed—provided the right incentives and price structures are in place. However, it is essential that substantial support also be provided by the public sector (notwithstanding the serious resource constraints confronting many countries) and by the international community.

Current climate-related financial flows—including funding provided through the Global Environment Facility, the World Bank, the Clean Development Mechanism, and bilateral assistance—are far below what would be required even in the most optimistic scenarios. Flows to African countries, small island developing States, and least developed countries are particularly low. Although new initiatives have been introduced and additional funding promised, international commitments with regard to the provision of financing and technology support to address climate change remain inadequate and must be urgently reviewed.

At present, the mechanism for transferring financial resources to developing countries to help them combat climate change is based on the cap-and-trade system and, in effect, relies on market forces to determine the price of carbon and the market for certified emission reductions (CERs). There is, however, very little agreement about what the price of carbon should be or, more accurately, about its cost to society as measured by the marginal impact of the emission of one ton of carbon. This lack of agreement is understandable, given the wide range of projections on the impact of climate change and the costs of reducing global emissions. In a survey of one hundred estimates of the social cost of carbon, values ranged from US$ -10 (indicating a net benefit from carbon emissions) to US$ 350 per ton.[23] Carbon markets have been criticized for being very volatile. Often cited in this regard is the experience of the most advanced market, the European Union Greenhouse Gas Emission Trading Scheme. As shown in figure 4, when it became clear that too many permits had been issued by the Europeans in the spring of 2006, their value declined sharply.

---

23   Intergovernmental Panel on Climate Change, "Summary for policymakers", in *Climate Change 2007: Impacts, Adaptation and Vulnerability—Contribution of Working Group II to the Fourth Assessment Report of the Intergovernmental Panel on Climate Change*, M.L. Parry and others, editors (Cambridge, United Kingdom: Cambridge University Press, 2007), available from http://www.ipcc.ch/pdf/assessment-report/ar4/wg2/ar4-wg2-spm.pdf.

Figure 4
European Union allowance prices and volumes traded, February 2006-January 2007

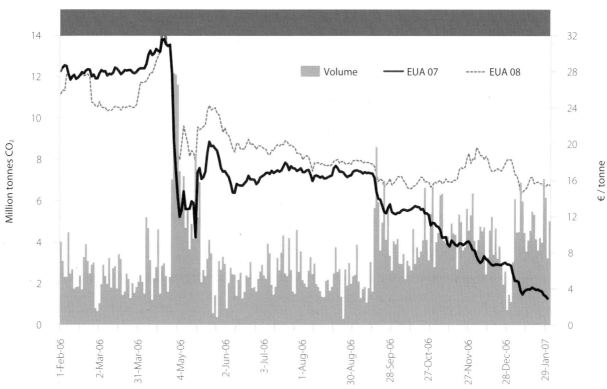

Source: Erik Haites, "Carbon markets" (20 August 2007).

The Clean Development Mechanism, set up in accordance with the provisions of article 12 of the Kyoto Protocol, will likely be expanded over time, and there are indications that it could serve as a vehicle for transferring hundreds of billions of dollars to developing countries.[24] Just under 235 million CERs had been issued by mid-December 2008, and it is expected that 1.37 billion credits will be issued by the end of 2012.[25]

---

[24] The Clean Development Mechanism "allows emission-reduction (or emission removal) projects in developing countries to earn certified emission reduction (CER) credits, each equivalent to one ton of CO_2. These CERs can be traded and sold, and used by industrialized countries to meet a part of their emission reduction targets under the Kyoto Protocol" (http://cdm.unfccc.int/about/index.html).

[25] Statistics obtained from the United Nations Framework Convention on Climate Change website (http://cdm.unfccc.int/index.html) on 21 December 2008.

An estimated US\$ 7 billion was invested in projects registered during 2006, with most of the funds (US\$ 5.7 billion) directed towards projects incorporating renewable sources of energy and improved energy efficiency. Investments in projects that entered the Clean Development Mechanism pipeline in 2006 were estimated at some US\$ 26 billion.[26]

Wide-ranging financial expertise and an understanding of sophisticated financial procedures are needed for countries to take full advantage of the expanding carbon market. Clearly, the larger and more institutionally advanced developing countries are best positioned to tap into the Clean Development Mechanism, as evidenced by the fact that half of the capital invested in the projects registered in 2006 was concentrated in three countries—Brazil, China and India. For developing countries lacking the institutions and infrastructure needed to secure project funding within this framework, assistance will be required. It is often these countries that rely on the most rudimentary sources of energy, such as cow dung or firewood; where such a situation prevails, assistance efforts should focus on expanding indigenous energy production in a way that allows them to skip the fossil-fuel-based development path pursued by industrialized countries and shift directly to clean energy. In this context, as in many others, the financial and technological aspects of sustainable development are intertwined.

International cooperation in technology and trade

Developing countries will not be able to adopt clean and efficient energy technologies until barriers to access are removed, as called for in the Bali Action Plan. Such barriers include cost factors, institutional obstacles, and legal impediments.

As mentioned previously, the cost of alternative technologies remains high. While costs are expected to decline with advances in technology and economies of scale, they will be high enough in the short run to prevent some countries from considering alternative energy options viable.

Another important challenge relates to institutional readiness. While the need for technology transfer has been emphasized in a succession

---

26   Erik Haites, "Carbon markets", a paper prepared for the Secretariat of the United Nations Framework Convention on Climate Change (20 August 2007).

of international agreements, there has been very little concrete progress; in particular, little has been done to identify the nature and extent of the institutional changes that would be needed within developing countries to facilitate the adoption and development of the necessary technologies.

Among the legal impediments that might restrict access to certain energy technologies is the global intellectual property rights regime. The Agreement on Trade-Related Aspects of Intellectual Property Rights (TRIPS) and other such instruments may need to be revisited to ensure that clean energy technologies remain accessible and affordable.

Policy coherence towards sustainable development

The Bali Action Plan, in operative paragraph 1(b)(vi), urges consideration of the social and economic impact of response measures within the context of enhancing national and international climate change mitigation efforts. The emerging literature on policy coherence offers a useful and transparent framework for assessing this impact, highlighting the need for developed countries to ensure that aid, trade, security, immigration, environment and other policies that affect sustainable development in poorer countries reinforce each other rather than working at cross-purposes.

The countries of the European Union and a number of other States have established mechanisms designed to bring greater coherence to their suite of global sustainable development policies. For example, emission targets for Annex I Parties have led to the adoption of national policies and concerted investment in new institutions, most notably the emerging carbon market. However, the implications of these policy and institutional choices for the sustainable development agenda in developing countries have not been systematically addressed. There is an urgent need to evaluate such choices on the basis of objective development criteria and to identify mechanisms that will help ensure greater coherence between climate and development policies within and among industrialized countries.

Conclusions and recommendations

Achieving the Millennium Development Goals, including the targets for environmental sustainability, requires adequate funding as well as technology development, transfer and dissemination. Greater coherence between the climate and development policies of industrialized countries will help to move this process forward.

Sustainable development prospects in developing countries are influenced by the direct impact of climate change, by the spillover effects of climate-related policies in industrialized countries, and by the repercussions of adaptation and mitigation activities in the developing countries themselves. Sustainable development policies in all countries must be formulated with due consideration of this three-dimensional threat and its implications for adaptation, mitigation, and international cooperation and policy coherence—the key components of international climate agreements.

Adapting to climate change is critical for sustainable development. Steps must be taken to strengthen the adaptive capacity of policy makers and local decision makers and to empower communities, especially in the least developed countries. It is also essential that adaptation be mainstreamed into sectoral and national planning processes; among other things, relevant provisions should be integrated into Poverty Reduction Strategy Papers, fiscal space must be created to ensure that the necessary investments are made, and the potential adverse effects of climate change need to be taken into account in macroeconomic projections.

In line with the provisions of the Bali Action Plan, mitigation efforts are to be undertaken by all countries and will be guided by the principle of common but differentiated responsibilities. Among the industrialized countries, a coherent approach to mitigation has begun to emerge; this group has by and large opted for a cap-and-trade system whereby carbon emissions are assigned an exchange value rather than being taxed. This market approach has been supplemented by incentives, regulations, and direct Government investment in research and development. For developing countries such a strategy may not be ideal, nor does it seem fair or desirable to force these countries to reshape their plans to fit within the procrustean framework established by Annex I Parties. Although the carbon market is often seen as a means of strengthening and updating the energy sector in the developing world, the pool of potential beneficiaries is very small at present, as low-income countries typically lack the financial expertise and institutional capacity needed to take advantage of any opportunities that might arise within this context.

An investment-based approach that encourages the use of renewable energy alternatives appears to be the most promising mitigation strategy for developing countries. Those countries that rely primarily on traditional energy sources rather than fossil fuels should be provided with targeted assistance that will allow them to shift directly to clean energy technologies.

The investment-based approach to mitigation incorporates technology support, the adoption of regulatory instruments, and research and education, all of which strengthen the institutional foundations for sustainable development. To facilitate this process, urgent consideration needs to be given to the establishment of large-scale global funds to finance the transfer of technology required for mitigation and to help countries cover adaptation costs.

Litho in United Nations, New York
08-60197—January 2009—2,455
ISBN 978-92-1-104592-5

United Nations publication
Sales No. E.08.II.A.16
Copyright © United Nations, 2009